The Movie At The Back Of My Mind

Barbara Clark

The Movie At The Back Of My Mind

Viaduct Publishing ~ New York ~ 2019

Author electronic mail address: barbaraclark249@gmail.com

Cover and inside book design by Maggie Cousins
www.maggiecousins.com

Cover painting by Barbara Clark, *On Stage*

Paintings inside book by Barbara Clark:
Inscriptions, title page
Christ And The Apostles, p. 34
Chinese Teahouse in Forest, p. 60
Nile Journey, p. 66
Earth is Saying Goodbye, p. 81
Blue Moon on Arctic Glacier, p. 87

Explore these and more paintings by Barbara Clark:
www.barbaraclarkpaintings.com

Publisher's Cataloging~in~Publication Data

Names: Clark, Barbara Ann, author
Title: The Movie at the back of my mind / Barbara Clark.
Description: New York, NY: Viaduct Publishing, 2019
Identifiers: LCCN 2018915157 | ISBN 978~1727530247
Subjects: LCSH Poetry, American. | BISAC POETRY / General | POETRY /
Women authors
Classification: LCC PS3603.L35552 M68 2019| DDC 813.6--dc23

In memory of my loving grandmother, Ida Haimowitz,

who brought all her love and art into my life.

With all my appreciation I thank the two major contributors

to the birth of this work, Terry Hauptman, painter and poet,

and Heidi Russell, fine art photographer

and creative collaborator.

Introduction

In 1991, I was invited to Barbara's home for Portobello mushrooms, basil,cheese, and wine. We read poetry into the night and later, in my apartment on Silver Street in Albuquerque, we continued our reading into the dawn. I was mesmerized by her narrative depth and the breadth of her world vision. Haunted by her poems that symbolically portray a world of despair yearning for freedom, I always return to their radiant beauty and moral intelligence which make her work unique.

The Movie at The Back of My Mind, poems 1960–2017, presents a mature voice devastated by war and political violence that in her art is transformed into a means to still celebrate our chaotic world.The beauty of her words lie in the power of her images and the ancient/modern incandescence of her song.

This volume is divided into two sections each lyrically criss-crossing her engagement with art, literature, nature, love and loss. Sanctifying Etruscan art, Doestoevsky, Amelia Earhart and Sor Juana Ines de la Cruz, among others, they rise into the beauty of their own particular lives:

> I have been given a planet that is mine
> I pull together its threads--
> like any woman before and after
> fixing my eyes on myself
> for the first time   I become mysterious
>   and familiar.
>   ("Amelia Earhart")

Often the sea is the background of her work; she is drawn to its tempests that mirror those of the human condition:

> Nothing makes sense--
> to think of you
> to be washed by the sea
> ancient, formless, aching
> to swim backwards
> murmuring your name
> while you radiant, shimmering like the moon
> come naked into the seething cold sea
> hungry to plunge and cut clear
> of the wave and break on me.
>
> ("Not Remembering You")

Other poems turn upon themselves as she transforms geographies and histories bringing them into our lives now----Sor Juana refers to forbidden love but not of our time:

> The woman who loves women
> dreams of Sor Juana who lived
> too early to openly love women
> to praise them to touch them
> to sing Aves with them and watch birds
> leap into the highest notes
> with passion's grace and thrust freely given
> in this beating of wings, but not to her.
>
> ("Sor Juana Inès de la Cruz")

In the book's second section, "Sitting With Rilke" there is the deep connection to his Duino Elegies inspired by his famous lines, "Who,if I cried out,would hear me among the Angelic orders---".The images and questions are as one: the mysteries of our place here are of a tragic vision but an accepting one ending with the physical force of the last line:
"---and oh, the rush of wings." Her meditation on this question is her poem.

> Why should we all be here?
> Ice wind and silence. This was the destination
> I had discovered in dreams and saw
> we dead lay piled like animal hides
> used and to be used again
> each held a smile as if at the last moment
> they had entered the angelic orders.
> ("Sitting With Rilke")

Barbara's erotic metaphysical images are extravagantly resonant and mark her as one of the most interesting poets of her generation. I invite you to experience this moving poetic journey.

--Terry Hauptman, (PhD)
Poet/Painter

Inscription

The Movie At The Back Of My Mind

The Movie At the Back of My Mind

In my long memory which I can not lose
I see you against the spruce
Then floating between the sunflowers;
Your smile falls into the leaves
You pick it up   run on
The oaks are waiting dark covers you
But your smile burns through them
You hold it up   they shudder from its heat,
They have been so cold.
I have been asleep you have
Dreamed us awake there is a cry
Yours? Suddenly the whole sky
Massed blue and white comes at me,
The trees are flat broken
Your smile is light burning over all
It has the power of wings
Is Its own flight.
Can you follow--------

        I keeled down at my heart
        With so much to say,
        But I have
        In this memory lost your eyes.
        At the horizon's point I am
        As bewildered as the suddenly
        Ending trees whose branches
        Have disarranged the sky.
        Everything is touching
        We are holding each other
        Great rifts darken us when we

                    Forget this the sky is clearer
                    For my hand held against it.
I acted quickly came toward you,
As you stepped away the syllables
Were getting indistinct the day
Was exploding singing you held
Its fragments in your hand I said,
Come, we are going to move without
Effort we have lost our names.
Your pulse flays my hand we have
Learned to stare at each other
While the terror mounts. I am
Afraid and naked the poles
Are passing through me.
My blood's spectrum guides us
Like phospor across continents
Whose trees follow their roots
Billowing in air. Your smile
Is on my arm.

Suddenly we see the movie called
Earth someone is making it as we
Watch I am being born raw and late.
My mother lets go you are in the room
Older than you are now.
Your smile burns my shut face
Then I start to talk telling you,
Wait leave the room,
I must hide till later when we
See the same trees
And the sunflowers in the dream

That is our birth.
Later we are more than born our veins
Run with gold the seeds the trees prick at us
Seeming to grow forever.
Stacked up between silences
An alphabet hums through us
Enormous grief's with no place
To go await its words to escape.

      We see the earth moving
      The film follows.
      Keep clear I know that land traps
      Do not move your mouth
      On it.
      Look towards me--
      In a great rift filled with light
      I am dreaming the trees are blue
      Floating over me sunflowers
      Hoist themselves into the sky.
      I count and count suddenly
      Your smile waves its hand the light
      Stiffens into a crystal rope
      Muzzling me instead of breath
      Slivers of time race
      Into my throat.

We are always having imaginary conversations

I am going through water at breakneck speed
come on shoals collide am shipwrecked and my blood leaks
through the telephone wires-
  we are still talking
  I become white
  you say your hands are growing
  large and red our voices continue
  the sea is beating into my lungs
  you say I sound muffled and your throat
  begins to hurt from so many words
  especially now your hands are pulling
  at the cord we never spoke so clearly
  I am at the center the birds jet down
  searching pieces of the wreck
  the rocks shift as the waves hit
  and seeing me in the madding surf
  they pressure the sky-
  I am white like salt
  leave me I cry I am having
  a conversation I am not yet your food,
  but you have eaten me and grown large
  blood choked I drink your strange syllables
  and seeing me on the rock the cord moves through the water
  it is your way of reaching me
  as I am shipwrecked my parts
  scattered on the seething reef.
  My breaking was like a knife scoring
  what I thought was always mine -
  a wrong memory---then I ask you---what is the food

of this conversation—is it love?
        You will not answer--
In the hollows of my body I feel the sea stretch
like a skin holding to me and in its giant ribs
through which the tides break your cord
rips away   I am green again.
Spellbound I come on shore to a sun
whose burning eye holds me there in silence-
a true conversation.

Genesis

Went to the dark mind
    and was very brave--
saw youth like clover spread across the field
    a green skullcap fastened
to the mending earth wet
with intercourse the audible grass
rolling its hands forwards backwards
    as they cried blazed in their sex.
They would couple and lie open to the beasts
    come to take them
    come to take them in the field
then went into the dark mind with love
was murmuring "come to take them"
on green mists weaving into their
      naked embrace-------
        Animal shudders
  the rising of beasts
 fur hair mixing a green skullcap
    Eden's promise youth
in a field now making love
    I felt it
    I thought this current that moves us
is the first star breaking
    on its own waves old waves
and spreads out the galaxies--
    such patience in the dark mind
to make us very young
    to make us very old

to circle us in our cries then
    silence us.
Went down to the field changed
    skin and mixed with beasts
 who cried out as we came
        to take them
and was very brave parting from myself.

At Night

Hoping that you survive the night I sleep
holding your wrist as it trembles against your mouth
and you whimper trying to leave the blows
they give the years they take.
Your masters never die.
In your dream there never is a sky
the sun wanting a better sight tears away,
everything is black—only the smells gutter
like manic flames.   Some nights
when you are desperate your dreams
invade mine—willingly I let you guide me--
I tell you there is nothing here that is yours
but you take me further no command stops you
from stumbling to that place where the cold
picks at your bones on the splintered floor.
You stop lie down wait for them to call--
I call your name you moan as if I am battle
your arms flail at the wood banging banging
your mouth moves a strange tongue
into the air's raw nerves. When you suffer this
I am never frightened—witness and lover
I am completely yours.
One night I will go alone,unexpected, sucking
into me their chambers graves barracks
where waiting they see their own nightmare tilted
draining blood their uniform's rot
becoming skin and face. I am in them
for their death for alone without orders
they are gravediggers;

full circuit and gone from your night
they will march to the cells   past the mounds
of a million sleepless nights
of measured chaos and never marching into hell
they will be left corpses eternal whose bodies
like a scum seal off the past.

Quarrel

..........................the air weighs in the balance

the stones

wall themselves away

a gradual movement and the trees

are back in place

nothing scheduled today

slight dispute with our memories

hair in great tufts torn out

now it is a definition of circumstance

I love you

the sand hits the wind

invisibly the air bleeds..........

Love, O Careless Love

"----------------the trouble with love
is that you have to believe in it,
like swimming ------you have to keep it up."
                              Louis Simpson

They met and it was love
But not at first sight instead
It was at night by touch
They fell in love. They were free to think----
"This is forever—time will pass but not
Across her body or mine---here, the air
Is pure, the walls protect
And the sleep we have
Comes only after love. For we
Are at the still point of love
Transfigured in a darkness
That is light-----our kisses
Mysterious as immortality."
        They shocked each other
         With their love,
         Their passion, the cries that tore
         Their bodies and made them one.
         What you would call, "a deathless embrace".
"Time will pass but not across
 Her body or mine."
That's the problem with love
It promises infinity
It reeks of it and then, then

The walls do fall away
The mouth has said too much
Or not enough
And the great sorrow is ultimately
They reach the future
That too–definite space
And the blow they take
They take alone.

       O Love, o careless love
       At the wrong time   you
       Collapse around us
       And yes, I ache to say time
       Did pass across her body and mine
       Taking us to an older part of earth
       That labyrinth come from loss-
       Slow river drifting on our
       Heart's current until
       We disappear.
       Who could explain what happened--
       The door broken-
       O love, o careless love.

"I knew you would always talk"

I knew you would always talk
even when naked you spoke-
on the bed   against the sheets
your mouth on the pillow still speaking
you pulled the covers   and I saw words,
when we ate   in front of the candles
over the plates murmurs passed between us
the knife heard   and the syllables
stretched deeper as we began to finish
if we could get to the street
there was more to say
into the wind and around the corner
we carried whole sentences,

      against my coat
      the nouns burned flew
      we waged words I knew
      you never meant me harm
      but this was speech without love-

  I fell----you asked, "How will you get up
  from a pavement broken by verbs?"
  Such rigorous language such
  awareness of enigmas—and as I lay there blood
  like wet pollen framing my mouth I gasped to
  answer you but you were gone
  and on the street had left
  a paragraph it hung on air clutching
  the buildings---
  you spoke well your phrases

made me tremble   I loved your thought
so deftly carried to its end-
I knew it frightened me
its elevations of sound   its storms
the breaking of rocks
underneath the absolute zero
of all our words.

"I am in the sea father"

I am in the sea father
a dark horse trembling in the sea, father
I am covered in knives father
and you see me but the water
is too harsh the spray blurs
you do not recognize your daughter
her hooves striking foam
father, I am in the sea
salt cakes my eyes I beat & go under
my mane ribbed in blood moving
to shore-----you're calling incendiary words-
      "come closer ------am I your enemy"
in this phosphorescent music we are not laughing
we are not singing my blood comes closer
making you smile I think I have never seen you
so fierce to wave goodbye a gust of hands
tide after tide pushes back as I come closer
am I your enemy----
salt-stunned & caught we are drowning
on different shores no element holds us
me a dark sea spins like a shell
your land walks over you
no roots prove we were hooves
footsteps blood fragment of beach
eyes burn out the world....
          hear me
          I am in the sea father
          trembling in the sea
          & covered father, with your knives........

Miracles

Water into wine bread and fishes multiplied
Incarnation shimmering on the waters
in feathers floating across the desert
to its dry edge where the sea startles
the parched world
and we rising with fingers and wings flexed
at the waiting sun break our hunger
and climbing from the rocks
walk on water
on the chill backs of fishes see our faces
our wings steady over the fields of water
the broad loaves of our hands filling
each other incandescence a sun-god above us
Jerusalem in the sky no memory of hunger
the cold wind stirring the night--
locked out once we do not go again
to that place but in the journey
of wine and bread we pasture ourselves
in the sea the rough clothes turned
to feathers or scales or flesh
three into one and so sharing we call---
eat, eat of the growing that comes
from our blood
this incarnation steadies the water--
the desert breaks
its rocks into fire
we are multiplied -

16

In Arkansas

As she is leaving
her dress caught
in an arkansas field
she is in flame,
I am, too, hearing
her words speak
without her
by the lost farm stove
in a kitchen where memory
is the eternal meal---
       she holds an old hand
       that takes her to the rough pasture
       of whittled grass and fragrant suns
       where wild flowers spume across the wind
       and as she squints her child's eyes to see
       where he points the outlined world
       given her in its sheer muscle of birth
       floods her genital darkness and she begins,
remembers, cries-----she knows the horizon breaks
when her bright father corners her
with his two-fisted dreams

       But now an old man talks her
       to his world's center
       its clear lens of yellow and blue
       washed by rain, a rush of love
         and she is in an arkansas field caught,
         scrubbed winds ploughing at her heart

as the space he gave goes hard
in its grief and her father's hum
tells of the child unshielded
from his heat------
her naked eyes bend to raise the woman
whose body has caught tears her dress
blackening in an ancient sun while the child is borne
again into the old mystery
where the stove shudders
her into peace
and she sits hearing
how she was loved,
summer in her lap.
When I see you so slight and alone
 waiting for the hand to go away
I would tell you
that field is in your heart
never going
and when you choose to run
the wind's your feast----
come, the field has ripened,
the sun's old hands forge
the world and we are growing
in our green souls
toward light,
    there is no burden left.

Distances

I rub two sticks for fire
nothing----------
I rub again the wood is dry
slight wires of smoke spume
from my hands then nothing
I am living in a wood stricken
by cold I was born here
where else do I become warm---
       the telephone rings
       and my room starts
       to grow sound pushes
       the walls apart cracks widen
       and out of the wall is a ringing -
       I am keeping faith with you
       hearing unmoving calling
In the country
I remember the doe trembling in sunlight
at the pine's edge I asked you not to fire
but you laughed------"there is a proper way
to ask for mercy" she fell a denseness
of beauty the earth wheeled
wild needles spun around her
    I went
put my hand in the blood marked
my face.........in all directions winter sun
    and snow we are in a wilderness
    and there is such longing for death
     but properly asked-----

why did you bring me to this?
The room you left me was small
"I will come back" you fled
began then the legendary waiting
the blindness hunger
and outside the fields were burning,
the poor, sweating in their circles of fire,
brazened the winter like animals crouched
in a make-shift purgatory---
  I put my hand to the window
  the numb years in my fingers
  trying to get out I know we
  are all trying to get out-
  across the cold pane
  it is time I watch
  cutting deep
  in that child who lost
  gravity space love
  and lives with the dead
  free in her mind.....
      The first cold ripples the pavement
      and silent cells that bear me
      work harder against what is lost
      the trees giving way become bone
      meditative in their stunned skeletons
      my hand slides falls off "yes"
      onto the chill bark whose cells
      work harder against the hackles of cold---
branches scavenge the air for ballast
not to fall
a paralytic sun stands over my head

not to fall
and I seeing my own self shining
out of time a hostage to boundaries
have gone distances where everything
remembered in the dark windless glare
of this life has been not to fall.

In Memory of My Mother

In the morning I went somewhere--
I knew you were dead
and the time was coming
when you would be dead again-
I flew away so light and landed
on a tree heavy with snow
it did not feel me. There I watched
you rise from your sleep
in the tumbled earth and walk
slowly down the winter streets
so familiar you could not think
you had ever gone.

        No one saw you walking
        and over snow and ice you left nothing.
        I could not call out.
        To have winter in the soul
        now, I understood.

Courage

I try to measure it,
in the morning it is small
pinched with dread   God knows
what I dreamt
to make it this way.
As I lift off the bed
talking to it
I swear I hear the pump
go on a large electric glitter
fills my brain
with courage.
I dress it's expanding
big red arterial flower--
courage courage
and it goes down into the coffee
which boils with fearlessness
my heart starts banging
like a strong oak staff,
thumping thumping
on the kitchen floor.
My breath beats its measure
and together I am light
a dirigible a swimmer flyer
courageous
       sailing out the door with courage
       courage my bird call
       wide-winged song
       great distances great heart
        immeasurable lift

into the blood-red clouds
they,too, have arteries
and pour themselves out
every morning no matter what.
Courage.

Homage to the Emperor Hadrian

"Animula, Vagula, Blandula
Hospes comesque corparis,-"
Soul of me, vague debonair,
Guest of this body and friend
"Quae nunc abibis in loca?
Say whither now thou wilt fare---"
                            --Hadrian's poem

On nights when I see light
in terror of the universe
My soul tells me,
"You must keep going,
 you must keep going"
Its whispers choked and harsh.
I ask:
"What will you bring to make me stay—
What eternal river will you carry me on?"
    "The coldest of rivers with laughter
    with death running its currents
    where you must be rough like stone
    stone hidden in fissures
    stone of boulders of comets burnt
    black and hard seamed with fire."

Soul, better than I, traveler, seer,
I want corals fruits seasons only
of spring of summer things warm
and inexhaustible----crystals fractured
by love and lunatic spasms of air

spinning into my words----
But you offer such a little suffering world
and that is a terrible food to eat.
"Nec et soles dabis locos"
All thy jests at an end.

A Song of Love & Despair----In Memory of Neruda

With too many poems
you went out to sea
you were drowning,
the water, acid,
on the shore I stay comforting you
writing love poems
and a song of despair-
    sobs like dust
    come out of my mouth
    as I wrap my words
    for burial.
I stay alive and forgetful
breeding orphans in my mind,
my thoughts go their own way,
and the streets I stand on,
the pen I write with:
    love and despair
    love and despair-
I go to the movies
in every film I see
I look deep in the water
watching it move in waves
over your body,
you lift and fall, lift
and fall, poems heave
from your chest and ribs
breathing out words,
fish gather in your mouth singing
flickering and swaying on the tides,

they are your songs
your rhythms spawning out
their lips I sob:
    love and despair
    love and despair
too many poems
you carried too many poems
into the sea----there is the love song
of the ships they go out of harbor
and anchoring where your body fell
glide magnetically over your death
hearing new songs rising
from the salt-spinning currents
that hum in your bones;
they will never desert you.
      on shore I stay writing,
      love songs vanish
      on the paper,
      my hand dissolves
      from the tenderness
      of my words,
      of love and despair so much
      is left.

"Fishes or stars burning between her thighs
Shadow of birds scarcely hiding her sex-------"
                    Octavio Paz

Delirious melting of over and under worlds
her sex hiding what could be peace
she moving there like an army in silver
bearing fishes & stars to witless victims
who sleeping with her fall into fire
holding the stopped moons in cratered hands;
this woman moving in dark flight over the shadowed bodies
consumes worlds bound & waiting
as she rides through mountains & waters
invading---invading---only the fishes & stars drift
as she takes us in fire----
the scarce birds hide in what remains--
            She is in her splendor islanded
            a miracle of worlds---burning crystals
            mists and heavy cries the rhythm
            of her thighs stopping moons as she is ridden
            as she rides her army in silver
            her army consumed broken in its peace.

My father thought only of cavalry
so passionate was he that child and marriage
were eclipsed when he felt the sun's delirium
in his body the horses' pace at the track
and met the swarms of gaming men
who ran from wives
and weekend sex leaving
the puzzled child who wondered flesh
of my flesh why not love me------

         Indian warriors ponies careening suns
         at meridians that beat the eyes into a scar
         I was too late for you the blue and yellow sins
         covered the derelict's push west-----
         I bought a sword and hid it in my bed
         the bed swirled
         my weapon had a memory the desert filled
         with a burning bush toward which I rode---alone
         no wife no child I with a fire
         that came out of memory
         traveler in time to violence life ecstasy
         and deaths given an enemy who let me be a man----

He lost----silk shirt in a bettor's parlor
he rattled in his freedom gained a horse fumbled
with the money then sat staring into the past
a lifetime kept this up "my habit's horses—chance--
the shuddering numbers I make into a system---no time"

         The mirrors tell you're getting old
         not one Geronimo has threatened you
         or bullet spent itself in bone---
         the actors take your part as more and more
         you stay in the dark reeling house where cameras

                    make war for lost men---
                        there is that arrow, again
                    the Indian falls,
                    and once more the pony soldier drops the flag---
                    all lessons in eternity   the horses
                    shoot around the bend and dust charges
                    like a demon into that crazed pack......
                            He found living half clear
                            and was prepared for sharper lights
                            than any artist god or sun has shown--
                            the racers went away the wife and child
                            were immortality the track became
                            too straight to see the end
Where are you now dear friend   father
I see you more when I sleep
you stand inside smile
and have the look that says
about to go away   I know
I always did   but dear ghost
        who headed you off,
        what stopped you in the streets------

Jeshua

If I knew what was to happen in Galilee
If I knew my future   our history
I would never have spoken out
  -never raised the dead-
    healed lepers-
    I never did.

Now in their fantasy
I am a God become three.
It was told I pursued my death
Knowing it was the plan   my scheme-
am I a scheming Jew
as they say Jews are?

I was crowned by pagans hoisted
into the sky brought into a new history,
I said nothing.

I am rabbi to the Gentiles
because of me their grief is never done.
They speak the Passion of their Lord, I,
the circumcised Jew, am that Lord.

The road was long thunder above the cross
Jerusalem a mirage flickering in the heat
all around chanting roaring crowds
undone by miracles wanting more-
    The Romans shining in armor
      laughing   waiting.

I stumbled birds took flight.
Already the stone had rolled back.
I tell you the earth is cold and presses
in on me----my winding sheet covers bone
I will never be found and heaven
is as lost as Eden..... O poor blind world broken
by the myth.   My pity is your resurrection.
      Father, my father save me
      My heart stutters your name-
          Adonai   Adonai-
A new world begins its history will erase us
and I am taken from my people.
In strange lands Jews whisper
but none whisper my name-
    Jeshua Jeshua   Oh how I ache to hear it.

Christ and the Apostles

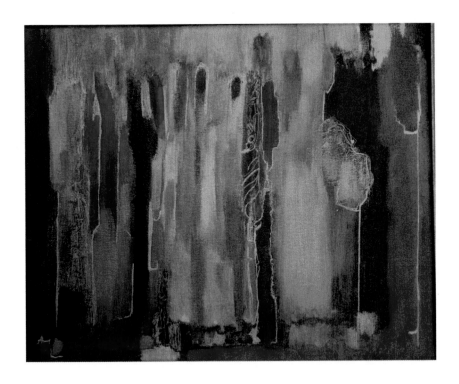

Wo wielest du....

Wo wielest du, mein yiddishe kinde?
Butchered, butchered in the starry night.
Why are you so silent in the chamber?
Butchered, butchered on a starry night.
Where are the children who never cry?
Why will no one take my hand-----
Wo wielest du, mein yiddishe kinde
Asking,asking chambers and stars
You've come too late to see where we are-------

An utter nihilist the sun

    gives up its rays

sees nothing trips across a table

    fractures its aureole scared as hell

        lies still

    and like a bad boy becomes

                a puddle----

the 21st Century begins---------------

Jacob's Memory

In the great ward of the chronic hospital
     remote, distant as the sun from birth
my father lay in the corpse of his body
     clawing the wrinkled sheets while the manic oxygen
straightened the rotted spine for one more breath.
     I screamed DIE when his mouth looked at me,
the worst of strangers; a shrunken memory in the lost cells
     jerking in the needle's spasm
under the red core of the whirlpool
     strangling the brittle foetus
coiled on the narrow bed.
     His rhythm of death reaches out
as I meet him in a dance of death and see
     a chain of hands, bodies tossed in the wind,
in a spring light jarred by roses and screeching grass
     until his body flies apart,crumbles to shards
of white flesh phosphorescent against my eyes
     burning me whole locked in the chair
where I see mortality zoned in cold
     and press my wrist on his to learn the last
minutes of time in the heart's articulation
     as darkness pours over the sheets
where I am bent to his breathing.

     Let me dream again, the spirit in that bloodstream is
     destined for stars:
     he goes alone and waits, a dead man in the Zodiac.
     He turns, he calls my soul goes in the dark
     crouches in the mute hostile blackness,

the dense sea of the universe stormy eternal -
he stumbles, cheeks staved in crying----
"I will die, I have died!"
We rush each other's nightmare
I shut my eyes,
"Oh, I'll hold you or we drown."
"Stop now!, the crab is in my groin;
It gains, my will is strangled in the cords you pull,
not even Time will struggle in me now;
I see the signs, how heaven's charts must turn:
I see the burning place they make for me."
The fever charts are broken
my roots twine in the tossed blanket
under the pillow emblemed with his hair.
I cast away silence in great leaps of panic
facing the savagery of the empty bed
where my conceiver shuddered in his wounds
I kiss his hand's failure to lift a glass,
to open windows for the sun and trap
the seasons counting out his life.
Here, now, take the darkness, dying, make it safe,
for when my flesh has edged away, shed me,
and I rise, my soul broken in its wounds—wait!
go into that future, time's flood and carnage
thrilling the memory,
pull yourself through its imponderable Hells;
go, father, estranged, fearful, go
there is not one who will not meet you
hushed in the blinding myth of death.

Israel After Borges

    ----a man who endures & is deathless
    & who now has returned to his battle
    to the violent light of victory
    handsome as a lion in the 12 o'clock sun--
              ---J.L.Borges

and the woman
   she is as handsome in the midnight
   when her eyes dissolve
   the iris going white as a cloud
   & she does not see the pyramids & the camps
   the old roads have crossed too much
   even her child she does not recognize
   it is too much a jew
            when she starts to go mad
in the soaring midnight she crosses the water
to the first desert where she burned
in the long robes & forging the sand
through her fingers screams
at the hard endless grains that never stop
that form neither mouth nor heart--
there is no child to be found
no resurrection in the sun's shed light
            as if in the womb there was a lie
& around the pits always always
stand the terrible black lions like men
who have no hands

Merciless Aesthetics
Venus After Botticelli

The way she stands the shell she's
    almost all atilt
full company of waves would take her
    if they could
and make her all the sea's.
    She'll ride it out
and knot the world for love.......
but till she does, that artist tempts the fates------
Hold still if she makes shore
that hairy naked angel dooms us
our beds will skid full sail,
the sea invade the streets,
& we're awash in legend no mercy shown,
it is too much to bear-------
       how can we like the way she stands--
       promised but unmet----

"O wave that broke out of the long dark nothing"
Come against me now take me from the shore
Sweeping my body into great hollows that plunge
With sea surge under the racing stars-
Let me forget that love has been lost
And boldness betrayed if I believe again
There is cause for breath and speech.

The first line of this poem is from Conrad Aiken's "Time in the Rock."

Directions to a Child in a Death Camp—1945

They were playing Brahms or Schubert
I said----Listen hard, this is
your last adventure see
how perfect the world can be hear
how clearly the sounds extend
past the nearest tree into the
nearest cloud---they were playing
Brahms or Schubert the musicians
held their instruments like living bodies
their hands closed on the notes
such strength before us---Listen
hard, I said this is your last
adventure when they call you
walk quickly before them the music
will still play think only
this will never end even now
the silence holds passages in space
Brahms or Schubert in waves circling us forever
perhaps near the sun by now.
Remember, art gives meaning;
when you go inside be aware
this is a fugue you enter,
your sounds will go forever--
be careful when you scream.

Remember love, ghosts look alike but the life
of the eyes demands the distinct object;
and where spectres are silent my ear's drum
must have sound like body's thuds and smackings,
primitive calls: see, my fingers unleashed
would make a point of telling you until
you groaned that I, your oppressive atom,
am faithfully writing one poem all my life...
unknown, unheard, it is about the sadness
of those thousand unseen bells that rang once
when you reached and noisily pulled
their tongues and you said, "yes...yes...".

For Miklos Radnoti
Hungarian Poet d.1944

My dear, because the mind is a fiction in time
you died, whether or not in July or on a
Friday, it makes no difference.
I write you a poem on a postcard charred
at the edges to show you, finally
the earth has been burned alive.
You would not want to see it.
          Darling, the world
leaks blood, even as I write
I cup my hands to catch
this human wine. We have filled ourselves
to end our every thirst----to end
ourselves. The farms the haystacks
you saw are memories.
After they shot you,
all over Hungary and Poland
I still smell the sweetness
of your hair.   In the cellars
the blackberries stay alive for you
but children peasants angels
you were right, the artillery
tossed them away.
As I write flies surround my mouth
filling my wounds
with their wings.

As we are human------

death and wounds are what we wait
lonely lovers soldiers at the gate.
life knows we did no wrong
we wore it out in song;
forgive us as our bodies bled
for all the spirit that we shed;
we go far off into an endless tide
strange tongues humming at our side--
dear friends forgive us this last escape
death and wounds-----we found our fate.
Come soon where there's no violence
only light, the heat of resurrected silence.

For the Tides, the Days

I could have been your first day
   and the morning of your first yes--
      forgetting all others
      I grow new flesh for you,
it rains
a heavy rain in an old house,
we start the solid air with speech-
like needles the rain and words
pierce in-
            all night next to you
            I forget all others,
            you tossed words
            into the morning and eased
            the last cup to your mouth
            and of what was taken I thought
            this is mine   I drank
            solid air like needles
            risking the end of my first sleep.
All dreams are a thirst
that in waking speak
we spoke the oceans were hungry
we gathered and were borne
from out the first house   and you
were in a chambered sea   unspeaking
swept on tides   I was salt
spinning in your mouth
you hearing how yes pierces
then hums along your throat   your breast
where I join you

and we are first in dark earth
in a house that owns morning and yes
and receives first what is ours.

Wordplay

There is the word "past"
  then the word
   "passing"
this last said while riding
  on a horse, in a car–
something quick of motion–
blurred trees are passing or
  we go past them
our eyes take in this incredible
  amount of motion–
then we are passing or we say,
  "hurry, our lives are passing us by!"
that word goes separately past us
  as if estranged from ourselves–
we have lives that go in different directions
  so that we stare at something–us–
    so quick of motion blurring our eyes
in that incredible amount of light.
      I went one place,
my life seemed to go another,
   going faster we
don't catch up the word catches up,
  "I passed myself going past."
   Irreconcilable selves.

Meditation

Breaks on our eyes the diagrammatic light
on the ceiling the waves spin
out of deep water   out of music
grown shadows come from evening
from childhood whispers etched
on sand   we hear at tidepool
wash and hoist of the sea knobbing
into the rocks grains tossed
extinguished like childhood--
                the ceiling shifts on the sand
                light flares on the waves,
                I am reaching beyond the tides.

Sitting With Rilke

Sitting with Rilke

"Wer, wenn ich schriee, hörte mich denn
aus der Engel Ordnungen?"   -Rilke-Duino Elegies

Who, when I cry out, will hear me-----
In my dream they were all around me
stacked like wood in the snow
I stumbled on them tripped
on leaves branches until I fell
I saw a face a smile a hand curled
eaten by its dead mouth.
        "Wer, wenn ich schriee
            hörte mich denn
     aus der Engel Ordnungen?"
I said to it the smile
        the face.
Why should we all be here?
Ice wind and silence. This was the destination
I had discovered in dreams and saw
we dead lay piled like animal hides
used and to be used again
each held a smile as if at the last moment
they had entered the angelic orders.
If this were so who would be left to wake
to fill the empty world if in sleep
we die and ascend peeling off our skin
and ease into oblivion the world no more
the heavens there just as we pretended.
        All around me lost light from the fading sun filters

onto the snow the white haze grows darker
the thickening woods listen as I walk on
blind sleeper.
Who when I cry out will awake with me
will say I have returned not gone
with them and am still sheathed
in this animal who breathes with a small
unsteady flame fragile in the insensate
   dark.
            The snow shudders floating into silence.
"Wer,wenn ich schriee--?"
         the rush of wings-
Banks of snow like sea-shoals glisten
in the moon's light.   Blindly I breathe
   into my dream.
If I could raise the dead and let them
 comfort me would I feel their wings rush
and sweep against me---would it be love's presence?
   Under my steps the snow's crust cracks
   like bones.   And they, they still smile
   wings and flesh trembling rising
   into a sky that shudders like a waiting
   lover impulsive restless.
   In my winding sheet I watch
    as wave upon wave the dead drift
   into the stars a living soul
    can not pursue them and across
   the planets they sign to me
   those phantoms of my night.
   My eyes close   I believe
   there is no grave

there is solitude
and oh, the rush
of wings.

Rilke-"Who, when I cry out will hear me among the Angelic Orders?"
Duino Elegies

St. Francis

Oh St. Francis no birds singing
and no animals to talk to in this wilderness
of neon flowers and aluminum trees...
so divine Italian ventriloquist when do you admit
it was a mistake or else you faked the vowels--
won't you say you never let your shoulders
branch the birds they fell and every beast you saw
was you---
if it's empty now it was empty then--
the truth! Or else we come from madness our bestiaries
swollen lies every imprint of hoof and broken wing
was fancy the zoos are empty.
What did you hear distracted Francis who understood
the mystic's heat who entered the verbal sky
and believed the beast's Latin--
Sweet Francis the dark murderous harbor in the breast
holds no myth the heaving blood path of this world
is silent what did you hear....not one cry
among the fountains or hoof scratching turf...
a vigil of emptiness the prey fleeing through time.
Francis chaos now makes us run the path of beasts
the insistent sky is empty smelling the new world
our hairs rise....
Mad Francis we fear the keepers and the cages
give conscience to our mind's shadow break us
nothing else is left
break us into spirit or flame.

Sor Juana Inès de la Cruz

The woman who loves woman
 dreams of Sor Juana who lived
  too early to openly love women
 to praise them   to touch them
 to sing Aves with them and watch birds
 leap into the highest notes
 with passion's grace and thrust   freely given
 in this beating of wings but not to her.

She dreams and tries to draw breath
as she sees Juana smoulder
in her devotions-
this woman of the cloth and rosaries--
and sees her float down
the hills-
crazy, a delirious nun with dark habits,
a dove who must light somewhere
in the stunned earth of Mexico.

Sor Juana 17th Century Spanish-Mexican nun, poet, philosopher,
scientist who was forced by the church to recant her secular interests.

O to love again
without pain
without desire
and inspire the other
to do the same---
a passionate tryst
without risk
each twisted to the other
in the shimmering dark--
spare nothing
indifference is the spark.

Meeting On P'eng Mountain

The scarlet birds on your robe fly away
as you part from me on P'eng mountain
not a word given of farewell...
Is it you I have, my long dark life,
loved.
Is it you, who like an early frost,
fell away on the fruit's skin,
holding my mouth in its icy flesh.

Chinese Teahouse in Forest

Li Po

Li Po must have been happy
drinking the way he did seeing the moon
in its phases catching it in the tenuous water
the stars breaking in his fingers
he must have shuddered at how clear
he was then plunged his wine into its mouth
so they singing together could join shadows
and forever drunk ride out the world.

Impressions of What is True

Shouldered by the sea I waited gleamed with sun
was ageless then time frightened me and I dreamed
empires on my eyes tested sea moonlight and
sun watched the sharp leap of crickets
felt the animals pace in cages where hunger
is forbidden crouched in a spell shaded until
the spectrum split its grains the elect stampeded
I was alone my enemies would not eat with me
I faded saw my hands my feet my clothes
leave enter life another way........
"I'm not going to last" but the antidote remembered
was lilacs lilacs moist in their perfumed city
where I dreamed the mockingbirds
sing all night-------
Love you know my secrets the frightening ritual
look of games that get up attack
travel through time that none can piece together
it is my summons to that Babel to those steps
covered by the sun's drift.

Not Remembering You

Not remembering you
I think of you everyday my days
drift against the sand the sand stabs
its crystals into the sea --
I watch as mortality
presses in on them
and without anger
each invades the other.
>Once I was of the sea
>taken by tides to places
>I never meant to go
>sent to shores where in moonlight
>I eddied round you
>you picked me up,
>held—then tossed me back into the sea.
How many times did I return
bringing gifts of seaweed tangled
in my hands   and always you threw
me to the tides.
>Nothing makes sense-
>to think of you
>to be washed by the sea
>ancient formless aching--
>to swim backwards
>murmuring your name
>while you radiant shimmering like the moon
>come naked into the seething cold sea
>hungry to plunge and cut clear
>of the wave and break on me.

After Actium

Cleopatra to Anthony after the lost battle

My eyes live in darkness
Chased by furies the sun goes down
Leaves pound into the earth;
Nothing will know our favor when we fail,
Captive to my hand and chamber
The world walked in   marshaled
Armies sparked the air
Clash of armor riveted
Death in our arms--
        O do not forgive me that battle I fled
Haunted animal, woman, prize
Of the world and not inviolate;
So it was I brought you
To this solitude and common desolation
Where silence crawls
In our flesh until our blood
Is plundered and time ends.
I hear the planets
Clash in the pit of the sky
Digging our grave, our tomb
Among the stars.
There is nothing in my soul but you
And in the world that waits,
I will come lie in your arms
And wish for other empires
To lose.

We shall not walk again on the shore
And watch the heron crying in the rushes.
Before us lies eternity
Our souls are love
And a continual farewell.

Nile Journey

Brilliant as she is...

Brilliant as she is, she lies in night unseen.
Her sex, her darkness, her body's flow
Electric where her carnal mouth is met;
He comes riddles her with light
She strangles midnight with a cry
        and she is darker yet.
Who wanted her that cries could be so deep
As night so dark inside its pauper's cell?
Mad woman whose rich body holds mad atoms
And the madder syllables of love,---she shifts,
Her breasts roar, tumble on the sheets, "My animals
Hold fugitive light, and bend it with burning claws
Until my lover thinks that dark is bright,
Until he wants me deeper
Than the thrust of light, as black is pitched
To highest vision on the night,
        where terrors have the keenest claws of sight."

The Deepest Memory is Of Life

There is a burning in the back of my mind
cinders and fumes like tears rise up
they are shooting the dogs snap
everyone screams but some laugh
the earth acts strangely as if the universe
had decomposed and a soft mucous
grids the field.
  In the long nights nothing stirs
  but the hoarse snow--
I am not dying as quickly as they want
I empty pockets steal throw
the dead onto wagons-----"Du lebst noch?"
and still my heart beats   I wait for you
I would not want you to know
my life hangs in doubt
I fear night and day
In the morning I wish for dark
when it comes fear waits for light.
  I would not want you to know
  I wait features retracted,
  catching myself in shallow breaths.
  Sirens come in the window
  My coffee goes black and acid.
  The day stares at its own peace,
  my eyes are folded everything is in place.
Nothing stirs but the hoarse snow
as the cinders float around us
marking our place.   Hunger and silence have mixed-
but I live my chairs my table lives   my flowers burn

in their colors and you which breath out of me
is yours   which eye scores the world waiting
out there   in the long nights nothing stirs
I'm out of range
the dogs are friendly---
    You are everywhere
    I will send this to you.

1918

I entered this century after a magnificent
War in which Death satisfied itself mightily
And the living offered themselves easily
Entering a scene they agreed to play.
Some were masters, some puppets,
All naked in the trench labyrinth.
Whoever believed in Heaven or Hell
Now witnessed more of Hell and prayed
Begging this insane passage
Be from death to life
That they not be stunned by shrapnel
Or twist moaning in the toxic hiss
Of gas clouds flooding yellow green
Like a malevolent sea into what remained
Of their throats.

> Lumps of men dirt clods heaped
> Breathing on each other
> Enemies haters comrades lovers
> Fitted to death
> Then planted in the earth.

I entered this century before the next
In which the undead came alive,
Rose from their graves remembering
How Death had no pity and so they,
Pitilessly came at the living
Who remembered them and if horror
Still held itself to a human face this time
It did not...It came from Hell
As some have said.

There were nights the moon was ice white
And days the sun did not rise:
It was no world we knew.
Men ran marched flew swept
Against each other—there were laws
No one lived by and the young exhilarated
Disfigured wielded Death the old
Grew fat filled with their own ageless
Particular hatreds ready for what they knew:
 Havoc and hallucination.
Still, some would not kill
And would be at peace- no matter-
Indiscriminate, the common grave
Moved on, taking a face a hand
The wallop of a laugh—all gone
And flesh whispered its wrath of memories,
Bodies rusted as bayonets pierced
The shredded flesh-
And the howling--- silent.
Everything has stopped sleep and wait
You will be called again
We have phantoms to meet.

The 1920's

I'm not born yet in Europe
People make their recovery
Drink up their memories
Lap up the Peace like a strange food
From a surreal planet,
And no one is any wiser,
Than before.

Men in great coats with humped backs
Floating legs, walk a foggy street
Or sit in a dismal bar. Hungry, poor
Not meant to last they will take
Their revenge---but not now.
To be ordinary is their wish
To avoid the cemetaries the memories
To recover a street a boulevard
Without mud covering bones
Or a lost arm or leg
Watching them.

For the others the civilized
Who stay unconscious
Paris is beautiful fragrant worth
All the death. Berlin is on the mend
Bands play chestnuts and lindens preen
In an icy sun over cafes where everyone
Is recovering gorging on the Peace that slides
Into the great rivers of Hades.
        But memory has its own soul and will not be lost.

Soon, when the soldiers, massed and silent fix
On their heads a helmet like a molten carapace,
And begin their climb back to the upper world,
I will arrive.
Forgive me for knowing this.

1939

In that summer of 1939
I am sitting on the beach
waiting for the chills to shiver
out of my body before I run
under the waves.
           I look back,
all is calm in my peaceful world,
it is not yet time for the bodies
to wash onto the beach for us to swim
between the charred wooden planks
floating to shore the sailor's clothing
clinging like splinters to the boards,
death's distress signals.
The milk of human kindness
is not yet sour though Europe
is souring on itself.
           This is my last hot safe summer.
Looking back I run again
and again into the water diving
waiting for one great glistening fish
to meet me instead a ribboned jellyfish
comes and stings I do not retreat
but dive deeper and twisting on my back
go under watching this phosphorescent
creature skim through the waves
before the sweeping tides
throw it on the sand.
           While Europe mobilizes
the sand runs through my fingers

and I wonder if I will ever again meet
the monsters of the deep,
go out so far where danger lurks and trust
the sea will hold me in its hands,
             --------------------and trust.
But I remember when the music stopped
and chaotic voices covered the air,
my father yelling, "Swim, come swimming, swim
for dear life. Let me show you how."
Doesn't he see the dead tied in their clothes
drifting in wave on wave
from the open sea-----------
Everyone laughs. It is night in Poland.
He is laughing close to tears. He will again
miss another war.

                So close to us the sun is ice white
                the jellyfish bleeds its colors
                into the sand the day is moving on
                and all those deaths are waiting.

In 1970 Richard Nixon authorized the American incursion into-
    Cambodia

In America we went into the hills
skidding on ice and gravel
as we climbed upwards, the snow
fading our hair flailing us
as we stood under its bite.
We saw the pond, a seared wound
where riddled ice festered in its ashen water,
the day we lost ourselves in Cambodia.

Wanting to be lost we struck deeper
bled clay into the snow, our footprints
hammered at the dream that anything
could be alive without a scar.
We were going higher losing the sky
in the storm then looked back
half seeing that other world where geese
prayed in their feathers, hovering on water,
the day we lost ourselves in Cambodia--
        and plunged on to beat and be beaten
for living in a secret country
where there are no screams and at the core
no feeling a dying world grown cruel its waves
of sleet flying stunning us the wind
wincing in its own salvos until the world ended.
The stones were shrouded from each other we stood
in a cold that grappled with our bodies our minds
so we could not remember whose words we should know
after we walked blood soaked

into Cambodia--
       here in the snow the sun bears down
on the dead the empty skulls scream in the wind
as we stare into the next century the day
we lost ourselves in Cambodia.

America 1972

In the midst of the burning we made love
wait till I grow up you said
then suddenly you went old
and I had you as we were dying in the smouldering street.

Everywhere the naked hold the roads
soldiers throw off uniforms and wait
we make love if they stay if not
we run at them until they do
this is their freest world---- I can not count
the times they said yes.

In the middle of the burning we made love
you said till I grow up wait
and then you went old
suddenly I had you in the smouldering street
we were like soldiers dying
wanting us to make love
while the naked held the roads
and the uniforms burned in the fierce cities
of the freest world we know.

The Last Call

The earth has become a science fiction movie
Fu Manchu and Alice in Wonderland
Have teamed up.
The Pod People walk around as crazed
as the rest of us.
I sit on West St. drinking
I don't know what,
it all tastes the same.
Around my feet there is water flowing
the chairs float they've evolved
to life at sea. I haven't I feel
wings of demonic size
erupting from my back bearing down on me
a burden from a source unknown.
My crimes and their footprints follow me.
From the river comes the thrashing of whales
They have lost their way.
"Save yourselves" I call or mouth
I can't hear myself no one is listening.
        The barren questions pile up.
            What provoked us
                What guided us—the great Golden
                shining ones the piles of stones
                the stench of incense
                the lost man ?
A world on the eve of its Crucifixion
not of the luminous Christ
far out alone unmoored shamed
by the blank stares of the unbelievers

Fu Manchu and Alice, yes,
they always knew---
snickering evil   savvy innocence.

Earth is Saying Goodbye

Your Russia

I tell you, Fyodor, with you light has never had a better landscape,
with you the pit went fire everything natural and illicit bound you:
super-bearded crimes and punishments, the necessity
of father against son, the sanctity of idiots-
your Russia a monastery of moral problems
the sleuth hounds barking over the Slavic heartland
carting home the stench of revolution in a droshky.
    As for me how many nights
    have the nihilists invaded come in the door
    when I tried to go underground;
    you could have saved me like the others,
    written into a book---
    without that I panic holding your pages
    there my strangest self goes unrecognized
    leaving me alone with it in life---
    I know one must give way to grief
    eating it down with onions
    washing it down with vodka.
In an epilepsy of soul shock I unspent my minutes,
unlike yours where much came back with consciousness--
I was stuck to my own palate but in your nest of fraternal
killers and women who become too vengeful
or remain innocent I would have found my fate.
I ache for cold and sweaty life at its last meal-
the deprived hearts splintered in drinking
floggings tears---your armed camp of a crazed species
would have been safe for me.
      I could have invented a crime

with real punishment written down
plotted out by you for me.
Talk to me, tell me no matter what--
 will you give me a story-
 Am I insane.

Late Age

I was already on the other side
and did not know for I had entered
the late poetry of great age.
Now I sit at an empty table
with nothing but oblivion
ask me and I will tell you
I have the courage to go on.

    I saved you a seat
    place yourself beside me
    be still as I turn the pages
    where my words fly away
    free of me at last.
    These stones we live on
    are my language held down
    heavy burnt by the sun
    which doesn't burn away my darkness
    that has its own color.

I was already on the other side
and in this late poetry
I write about the hiding places
of my own incurable beasts
the barbed wire that binds them
terrified keening at the ghosts that hover
when I remember my longing that floated
like a lost star over the night
and I look at the distance I have come
to be mortal.

BACH: THE PARTITAS

Phantom suns nightmare strokes the earth a dying sound
   thrusts the staves into the soul a wound music
silence and death the temporal plague exhausted time
  wearing the skin suns verticals of sound
   and the earth shifting in your fingers
his burning mind on your hands it is a light a feast
  the mind the ear for this was broken into channels......

   the grave and birth pause you hit
they start gain the boldest stretch of time
 nothing and of the upper air the weight the heat
the void insisting that we reflect how he obeyed
  the will of nothing yet plunged into sensual space
   possessed by the shades that live in music.....

   this trail has changed your hands as if your body
had by the sun been taken whole and passed to you--
  something wants you I hear it the battles and surrenders
his mind's victory lengthening on the board it leaps
  it leaps above the room makes electric solomon's hairs
   turns the pages of these books
sit still and bring it back your face bent to the bone
  tempered with your flesh that animal husk the bearer of sound---

he wills it to you the arches in space
  free-floating a devil's cathedral a silent guest the pain
   in the spirit of Johann Bach---
we wait to claim music's power
 wondering on the legend's of matter anxious to arrive

at the ghostly border coast of shipwrecks to meet
the hurler of suns who opens the waves dark rifts
and starts death and music from that same cataract
spun into the base of time------
Finish now
come from the keys as from a sleep inside the sea
the mind drifting to its resurrection a solar boat
loose among phantom suns   calls out hailing the gods.

Solomon—is the cat listening to the music.

Blue Moon on Arctic Glacier

Amelia Earhart

Rubbing her mouth against the horizon
  she thrusts herself out
on the libidinal currents,
woman alone the cell's hammer breaking skies
  her eyes and hands guiding the air
its membrane of breath winding in her
  as ribbed under steel and glass her heart
sheds itself over the hemispheres awake
  magnetic as she guides the world that sleeps
that cries under her pilot out of the rush of blood
  this woman who climbs through the sun's plasma
    calling your rays spill out my center
I am seed sucking your heat in me
new suns fire and the first living words
  as my mouth enters the incomplete world
swelling around me I am embryo whose form
  is finished and beginning----
the dials glowing numbers join me to this sky
  matrix of hair and skin the plane beats and cuts
    bearing me as high as the womb rooted
    in my flesh I move earth faster
than it has ever gone whole earth and sky
I have been given a planet that is mine
  I pull together its threads--
  like any woman before and after
    fixing my eyes on myself
For the first time I become mysterious
  and familiar.

After the Greek Anthology:
Betrayal

I waited for you
in that dark grove hidden in the mountains,
our place where only the owls watched,
        I waited for you.
They saw everything----our happiness,
our deep ancient touch, our cries.
They watched over us but then
    you left. They disappeared.
You lied to me, not to them--
my grief led me to strange places
where night air dense with smells
of rutting animals covered me
as I lay bare and shivering
    under Orion's hunt, waiting.
One day I saw a youth, like you,
tall, naked, skin the color of olives,
    so beautiful--
I ran to find you. Startled, he looked,
saw me, smiled & before I could speak,
he turned and shyly stepped off
    into the cornfield.

"I say by sorcery he got this isle;
from me he got it."

                                    Caliban

                    Prospero's Island

  One year since April on this island
 and I can not see you for time
   baited our innocence,
hooked it to memory,
Love's scenery in a world arrived
where distance ends.
                But master this
come to tempest's island where love and youth
share the mirror's husky gleam
with burning Caliban who, hand to throat,
staggers crushed by shadows.
            Lie down
in the beginning of the world where horses
mount the sand, their manes shaking from the sea,
and race into this island's scorched heart.
Come, make love where Caliban in his fever
roams the shore before the mystical horizon
of vanishing ships, bone and flesh locked
under the ravening sky's disjointed
pasture of reflected nightmare
where the towering black moors that change us
wait in the ruined world that is April.

The Dream of Reason Produces Monsters–

Goya: The Peninsular War - 1807

Gunshots in Goya voluminous clouds rifle the dream of reason
orders hunched in shoulders wrecked eyes behind the other world
stare out flesh hits canvas the piling dead thrust against the brush
red yellow green pure blends of death the fallen stare
seeing their blood tangling in the soldier's feet   and on the gibbet
what hangs stone-like and swollen is the lunging scream Kill
Attack Live!

> Goya make the masters follow knot
> the rich skin into the rope
> and as your brush goes down
> bulge their eyes with death's poverty
> take the sufferers away to a not yet
> part of the picture free them to gorge
> on wine the safe throat drinking it down
> let the women keep their children
> and what is wrong devoured
> as you take the soldiers' guns arc them
> into the officer's chest your brush
> ripping out his sword as everything
> cuts free rises out of the picture wine spilling
> uniforms undone wounds painted closed
> the maimed horses galloping while women
> cook the hideous watchful birds
> that lived inside the frame   as the dream of reason
> given to us at its height broken derelict
> hollowed out with its grief lies still
> and waits to devour us.

Lot's Wife

She was never heard from-never asked about anything. She was
a shadow woman from the Bible and no one begins to fathom-
why she looked back-there are no simple answers:curiosity,
rebelliousness, self indulgence—no, maybe it was the woman in her
refusing to believe a male voice saying she'd be turned to salt if she did
what she wished especially if he were directing the event.
But let us assume she could live happily in the negative,---that is, Sodom-

        Let me live in Sodom
          cleaner and straighter
       than the perfect cities
         of this world.
        Let me lie and cheat
          decently and forthrightly
         dignified to my end.
        Let Gomorrah be where I rest
          tended and healed
       from the perfect cities
         of this world.
        Let me nurse myself amidst evil,
          abusers thieves murderers.
        Let me watch as they curse
          the poisoned goodness
         of kindness, charity, tenderness.
        Let me use my fellow
          for my own ends—simple deceit
          guiltless violence-
        Let me love Cain, not Abel
          because Cain is the new planet
          because Abel unaware was slain
           by shrapnel in his chest
        and by us was all murder blest.

You Say------------

You say Christ has risen---has he?
Are you sure or don't you know--
Which is it ?
> Ninety years into this century
> braced on the edge of another
> the dead of innumerable wars
> surrounding every city oceans
> rivers fields covered
> with bones with screams
>> smoking the air--
>>> you say Christ
>> has risen are you sure or
>> don't you know---if he is he
>> eats bones señor—no better meal served
>> in this century,
> I am sure.

Grammar in Motion

Walks & legs go down the path
behind the bushes----a few words wait aimlessly
in the hot sun. I see them crisped & torn
light verbs that can not move & caught
in the black fence the nouns' moan
as their lips pitch against the metal
& where am I that as I walk I watch my legs
slide into sounds that stare at the sun
but have yet to come together.

On the Beach

I see that poor lady of the white hair,
that swimmer into death,
my mother,
she waves and calls
but in an ancient tongue
no one understands no one
rushes to save her I stand apart
and will not know this language
she once dragged out of me
but she stares and holds
my eyes the end of the world roars
around her. I am weeping and the great
clamor of salt in my heart cuts
her in two she was my enemy
ferocious and alone on her island
in the middle of my childhood--
she would not hear my solitary voice
how could I hear her ancient tongue
near the syllables of death--

       Oh death, death put seaweed in her hair
       before you drown her.....

Annunciation

Because she'd learned biology was destiny,
she knew someone had blundered, so---

in a rage she extracted her teeth
  she was very quiet as
all her body's parts floated before her lost
on the moving carpet that grew in every room
  her teeth flung on the floor   separated
slipping into the thighs that hovered
   between kitchen and bath
 her breasts each to a rib were alone
   she searched for her belly
 her taut vagina detached invaded
the shower sucking the water
   into its channels-----
her memory was on the carpet looking
   for the mind
that disowned it-------
    the whole articulation
     swollen with fear at the joints
        burst
    she bit deeply
her sinews scattered like long threads
   spinning and waving in air
tentacles of all she was----
   unmade.

And so it is true, biology has no
compassion.

America 2001 and on---

Fooling around with Death again,
I told you watch out it plays for keeps
 no hide and seek in the roses
no comic sugared Mexican death mask
 in greens reds melting on your mouth
     spotting your face   like a pox.............

Fooling around with Death again
putting your hands to your throat;
on your face Death's muzzle a rictus
around the mouth and no sound escapes;
the silent suicide you wake up
to kill your shadow to steal
your spirit your hands are always
cold.......
          I told you--
            I told

Billy Budd

God pounded
on the anvil of your throat
to let evil in the world.
Your voice moaned in its cords
like a ship in its rigging
and for that answer,
you were the guilty one.

In Memoriam

The papers say you're dead
but here there's nothing changed
no beds made   the chairs live well
and you have again   escaped your debts.

The papers say you're dead,
they purify my memory.
In the center of your tears
I watched you die;
the life you braced against still waits.
I live it stripped and bare.
No moving force   no clutter
the mirror steadily repeats the world
you lost   stars flame   the moon pries out
their shadows light harbors in half the world
and your pipe's decay grows bolder
in its dark metallic chambers.
Balanced in your space
I am witness at how easily
 our objects bear our death----
 the paper turns the page.

What is remembered

Where have I gone with you
covered in strange syllables
as a world flares around us,
gusts of fire holding our shadows-
where have I been with you--
a warmth a luxury of emptiness
as shadows caress our cries
arching their shapes over us.
    With you quicker faster than light
    the night's pulse spills into the world-
    Every night
    every night this incandescence
    piles fire on fire---
        Oh, what is remembered of that delight
        memory never old winged and brilliant
        and never old.

Love Among the Ruins---Etruria, Italy

Dangerous, dangerous, the Etruscans
who fill our room   will you leave with them
flowers of the ancient tongue filling
your mouth what melodies they breathe
into the springs of your music.
The goddess sifts her pollen
into the oldest burial bringing it to life,
so many bones and crimes
reliquaries holding the tissues
of their speech time so deliberate
so watchful   crouches in silence---
will you leave with them-

    Dangerous   dangerous to have loved them
    the lost Etruscans mysterious recumbent
    to have loved any dream--
    such a narrow hall in the chamber
    where you speak
    your words spinning on the cold stone
    carved stone   a woman's face listening
    she has a language that died before
    there is no food no fruit on her table
    but you speak insisting that she
    be life love after death-
    is there no one here who
    will love you--
        Do you see I am standing
        by your side.

The birds are still the flute player starts his melody
 the women heavy-lidded wait
Scorpions cling to their breasts crawling
along their lips and on the crumbled altar
I bring wine suns set over us our languages
are a caress weightless transparent--

It is dangerous dangerous
in the tombs living or dead
to love them their ancient speech,
she is a messenger who will never
reach you but you will hold
this woman dear who has been
scattered by time so silent
those thousands of years ago.

   By this table is the sea,
   the cold blue arena of the world pulsing
   in my hand my heart.
   Once nothing else was before love,
   before tombs lay the great solitude
   of the universe its liquid pollen
   swelling spawning its odyssey of blood
   so fluent, so fabled.

Flashes of distant lightning on the sea,
taut white slashes into the sky sharpen
then blur my vision and History in a burst of time
comes racing to me.

Falling Asleep Over The Aeneid

From no other look but what you cast towards me,
Fire inside, Troy burning in another woman;
Broken city where we loved.
Return-------
        Left in darkness I wait,
Touching your books and pen,
Your sword and robe in this room
That brings Paris to Helen again.
Do not change, be that to me
That storms the eyes of blind poets
As they hold the darkness with their words;
Hold me, golden and visionary
In this world's last night
As plunder and sword tear it apart.

epilogue

and so it has come to this
at end of day
i see galaxies bend their way
 into space
and the sun surging
 into another sky
as i go to lower

the bright flags of evening

Biographical Note

Barbara started writing poetry at an early age. Later her work merged with her interest in history so that many of her themes may be considered a "ghost archaeology", an attempt to use the past as a perpetual contemporary and, at times, a surreal presence. The forces of time and of love surface constantly in the poems. Her intent is to focus on different levels of awareness that allow memory and emotion to coalesce. Line breaks, spacing, and length reinforce this by relating the breathe of feelings present both now and then. At times this is achieved through a stream of consciousness which gives an immediacy to the life lived, remembered and sought after.

Included in this book are poems that are part of a long body of work dealing with the history of our wars—our past two centuries of conflicts which we joined or created. This is part of our ghostly archaeology and she questions how we can undo the eruptive violence with which we seem doomed to live. Perhaps poetry may help the living by undoing those future deaths to come and perhaps love will be heard and not lost.